My Best Friend
Martha Rodriguez

My Best Friend Martha Rodriguez

Meeting a Mexican-American Family

Dianne MacMillan and
Dorothy Freeman

Pictures by Warren Fricke

Julian Messner ⓜ New York

Text copyright © 1986 by Dianne MacMillan and Dorothy Freeman
Illustrations © 1986 by Warren Fricke
All rights reserved including the right to reproduction in whole or in part in any form.
Published by Julian Messner, A Division of Simon & Schuster, Inc.
Simon & Schuster Building, Rockefeller Center, 1230 Avenue of the Americas, New York, New York 10020.
JULIAN MESSNER and colophon are trademarks of Simon & Schuster, Inc.
Manufactured in the United States of America.
Design by Nina Tallarico

10 9 8 7 6 5 4 3 2 1

Library of Congress Cataloging in Publication Data

MacMillan, Dianne. My best friend, Martha Rodriguez.

Bibliography: p.   Summary: An American girl's friendship with a
Mexican American girl and her family introduces her to the holidays, games,
foods, songs, and family events of their culture. [1. Mexican
Americans—Social life and customs—Fiction. 2. Family life—Fiction.
3. Friendship—Fiction] I. Freeman, Dorothy Rhodes. II. Fricke, Warren.
III. Title.   PZ7.M2279My 1986   [Fic]   86-5342

ISBN: 0-671-61973-X

Acknowledgments

The authors would like to thank their
Mexican-American friends and professional
associates who helped in the preparation
of this book.

Contents

❁ 1 ❁
At Martha's House

Martha Rodriguez is my best friend. We both go to Monte Vista School in Santa Ana, California.

I like to walk home with her, but we always have to wait for her brother who's in kindergarten. I wish we didn't have to, but Martha says, "Javier is the youngest, and I have to take care of him." She says that her older brother Frank used to wait for her.

Sometimes I help Martha watch Javier. We take him to the park and push him on the swing. Javier doesn't like to do what Martha tells him. Once he got into a fight at school. Martha talked to Javier's teacher and then took him home.

I like to stop at Martha's house on my way home. I love to be there because her family is so much fun. Her sister Alicia, plays *La Lotería,* a game like Bingo, with us. She likes to play with us even though she is in junior high school. There are always lots of people visiting at

Martha's house. That's not like my house. I'm alone there until six o'clock when my mother comes home from work.

It's noisy at Martha's house when the television is on. Martha says channel thirty-four broadcasts in Spanish all day. Her brother Frank likes to listen to rock music on the radio while he studies. He goes to college. He says he's too busy to play games with us, but sometimes he helps us with our math homework.

The wall above the TV has pictures of Martha's family and the Virgin Mary on it. There's also a picture of her father in his army uniform. Martha calls it their "picture wall." I like to look at the baby pictures of Martha and her brothers and sister.

Martha's mother fixes Mexican hot chocolate for us. It has cinnamon in it. While she makes it, Martha and I sing the chocolate song:

Bate, bate, el chocolate,
(bah-TEH bah-TEH el choh-koh-LAH-teh)
Bate, bate, el chocolate.

Sometimes we get to use the wooden chocolate beater called a *molinillo* (moh-lee-NEE-yoh). Martha showed me how to twirl the beater between my hands and make the chocolate foam.

Martha's grandparents live on the next street and come over a lot. Martha's grandmother makes fresh

tortillas for us to eat with our hot chocolate. She rolls a ball of dough called *masa*. She pats the ball between her hands until it makes a thin round pancake and then cooks it quickly on a flat pan. Martha says her mother always asks her grandmother why she doesn't use the tortilla press. "Grandmother says she can do it better and faster with her hands. My mother gets tortillas at the store, but I like *Abuelita's* better."

Martha calls her grandmother *abuelita* and always speaks to her in Spanish. Her grandmother was born in Mexico. Martha says, "Abuelita is Mexicana." Martha was born in Santa Ana, California.

Martha's grandfather carves little toys out of wood. Once he made a toy flute and played music on it. He also plays a guitar that has a round back. It's called a *guitarrón*. He sings songs in Spanish. One of them is *"El Tecolote,"* The Owl. Each verse ends in *"Te cu ru cu,"* and Martha and I sing that part with him.

On Halloween, Martha and I went trick-or-treating. Javier and Alicia went with us. Then we went back to Martha's house to see what we had in our bags. Martha and I were dressed like skeletons.

"You look just right for the Day of the Dead," Mr. Rodriguez said. "In Mexico, on *El Día de los Muertos* we used to go to the cemetery to visit our dead relatives. We had a picnic and left food there for them. On Halloween the men and boys went house to house as you did tonight. At each house we sang songs to the dead, and were given drinks and food."

Martha's mother brought out a special bread. It was shaped like a man. Twists of bread dough decorated his vest and pants. "I bought this *pan de muertos* (bread of the dead) at the bakery," she said. She broke the bread into pieces and said, "Help yourself."

"Trick or treat!" Martha said. We both laughed as I ate one foot and Martha ate the other one.

❀ 2 ❀
The Birthday Party

Martha invited me to her birthday party. I could hardly wait. I knew that all her cousins, aunts, uncles, grandparents, and friends from the neighborhood would be at the party.

On the day of the party everyone was sitting in the backyard talking in Spanish and laughing. Martha's grandmother said, *"Buenos días, Caterina,"* to me. That's the way she says, "Hello Kathy." I answered, *"Buenos días, Abuelita."*

Martha took my hand and pulled me over to a man and a woman who were walking in the door. "I want you to meet my godparents Mr. and Mrs. Ramirez," she said. "I've told you about them."

"Feliz cumpleaños, chiquita." Mr. Ramirez hugged Martha and handed her a package wrapped in shiny gold paper.

"Thank you, *madrina* and *padrino*," Martha said, and turned toward me. "This is my friend Kathy."

Mr. Ramirez shook my hand, and Mrs. Ramirez said, "It's nice you can be here."

After they walked away I asked Martha what she had called them. "Those are special names for them because they're like parents. They baptised me, and they'll take care of me if I lose my parents."

"Hurry up Kathy," Javier said, "we're going to break the *piñata* (pee-NYAH-tah). I get to go first!"

"That's because he's the youngest," Martha said as she tied a blindfold on him and twirled him around.

The *piñata* was a large green and red rooster, hanging near the ceiling. I knew it was made of paper mâché. It had a long green crepe paper tail.

Javier swung at the rooster with a long stick and missed. Martha was next because it was her birthday. Alicia blindfolded her and spun her around. At first she hit the air with the stick and couldn't find the *piñata*. Then she hit only the rooster's tail. I saw why she missed. Two of Martha's uncles were standing on ladders and holding a rope between them. The *piñata* swung on the rope. They raised it out of reach when Martha tried to hit it. Finally one of the tall cousins had his turn and gave it a big whack. The *piñata* split open and candy spilled out. All the kids scrambled to get some.

Martha's father, her Uncle Ernesto, and her brother Frank began to play some music. Her father played the violin, and her uncle the trumpet, while Frank played his guitar. They're really good. On week-

ends they play *mariachi* (mar-ree-AH-chee) music at a Mexican restaurant. Everyone sang in Spanish. I knew the song, *"Cielito Lindo,"* because we learned it in school.

When Martha's mother brought out the birthday cake, her family sang *"Las Mañanitas,"* the Mexican birthday song. Alicia explained that in Mexico this song is sung to the birthday person as a serenade at sunrise. When Martha told me what it meant in English I was surprised because the words didn't say "happy birthday."

These are some of the words to the song:

Estas son las mañanitas,	These are the songs,
Que cantaba el Rey David,	That King David sang
Y a las muchachas bonitas	And to the pretty girls
Se las cantaba asi:	He sang this way:
Despierta mi bien despierta,	Awake, my love, awake,
	Look, it's already dawn;
Mira, que ya amanecío;	The birds are singing
Ya los pajaritos cantan,	And the moon has gone
Ya la luna se metió.	in.

We ate birthday cake and drank a red punch called *jamaica* (hah-mah-EE-kah), made from flower petals. Martha saw the face I made when I tasted the punch. She laughed and passed me the sugar.

While we ate, Frank teased Inez, one of their

cousins. "Just make sure, Inez, that I have a pretty girl to escort at your quinceañera (kin-SIN-nyer-ah)."

Inez laughed. "Don't worry, Frank. All my attendants will be pretty. You'll see."

I asked Martha what they were talking about. She explained that Inez would be fifteen on her next birthday. She'll have a special celebration called a *quinceañera*. "*Quince* in Spanish means fifteen," Martha said. "Frank and Alicia are going to be in the ceremony."

We played some games, and my favorite one was played like London Bridge. It's called Snake of the Sea. Martha said it in Spanish: *"Víbora, víbora de la mar, por aquí puede pasar."* (Snake, snake of the sea, here you can pass through.) Inez and her friend Gloria joined hands and made an arch. Everyone else lined up and grabbed onto the waist of the person in front. Then the line moved under the arch. The last player under the arch got caught.

Martha said it was the best birthday party she ever had. "I get to celebrate again on my saint's day in July," she said. "I'll go to church and give thanks to Saint Martha because I was named for her. My aunt Martha was named for her too. So we always celebrate our saint's day together."

❀ 3 ❀

A Sad Time

This week Martha didn't come to school. On Saturday I called her. She sounded kind of funny so I asked her if she was sick.

"I'm okay," she said, "but my grandfather died."

"Oh, Martha, I'm sorry," I said.

"It's all right, Kathy, he's with God. We're all helping my *abuelita*. My father says she's going to live with us. He said he's the oldest son so it's his duty to take care of her."

"Oh, when will you be back to school?"

"On Monday unless my family needs me."

Martha didn't come back to school until Wednesday. I asked her what she'd been doing at home.

"Well, first we went to the church for rosary for Abuelito and then to the funeral home. All our family and friends were there. My cousins from Mexico and Arizona came. We stayed there all day."

"All day?" I asked her.

"Well, almost. Uncle Ernesto took all us kids out for pizza. We were laughing and joking. Alicia said we shouldn't laugh with grandfather being dead. Uncle Ernesto said it was okay to laugh. He said Abuelito would like to know the family is together and laughing."

"What happened next?"

"I went back to see Abuelito. He was so still. I touched his face and said a prayer for him and said I hoped he would be happy with God. After the funeral some of my relatives stayed at our house. Alicia and I had to help with the meals. I set the table and washed millions of dishes. We also had to baby-sit for my younger cousins."

"How's your grandmother?" I asked.

"Abuelita is really sad, but she likes living with us. Frank and Javier gave her their room. Do you want to come over today?"

"Yes," I said. "I've really missed you."

❀ 4 ❀

A Celebration

One Sunday in December my mother and I went to Santa Ana Stadium. All the Catholic churches in Orange County, where we live, celebrate a mass there in honor of Our Lady of Guadalupe. She's the patron saint of Mexico.

Martha and I planned that we would sit together after we met inside the stadium. "My father and Frank are going to play with the *mariachis* in the procession," said Martha.

Just as we sat down we heard a blast of trumpets. A large statue of Our Lady of Guadalupe was carried into the stadium. Then came a high school marching band, dressed in red uniforms and tall white fur hats.

Then many people walked and danced by. Some of the women were wearing white blouses and green and red skirts with sequins. Others had on brightly colored embroidered dresses. The men wore white shirts and pants with red sashes. They were carrying Mexican flags and banners.

"Look over there!" Martha shouted. "There's my father and Frank." The *mariachis* walked around the stadium singing and playing their music. Their black jackets and pants were trimmed with silver buttons and braid that flashed in the sun. Frank waved at us as he walked by.

Dancers twirled to the music of rattles, flutes, and drums. "Those are *Matachine* (mah-tah-CHEE-neh) dancers," Mrs. Rodriguez explained. "In Mexico they're called soldiers of the Virgin." Their costumes were decorated with feathers and beadwork.

Then Martha and I shouted together, "The *charros* (CHAH-rrohs)." We clapped and cheered for the riders and their huge horses that pranced and side-stepped. The *charros'* clothes and saddles were covered with silver decorations. Wide-brimmed sombreros shaded their faces from the sun.

Choirs sang a beautiful hymn. The bishop went behind an altar surrounded by roses and began the mass.

Later as Martha and I walked out of the stadium we talked about all the other exciting things that were still going to happen in December. "It's my family's turn to celebrate *Las Posadas* next Saturday. My father said I could invite you. Can you come, Kathy?" Martha asked.

❀ 5 ❀
Las Posadas

When I asked my mother if I could go to *Las Posadas*, she said I could. She wanted to know more about what we'd do.

Martha explained, "We go to someone's house to ask for a place for Mary and Joseph to sleep. At first the people in the house say they have no room. Then after awhile, they say to come in. Only we don't say these things, we sing them."

I asked Martha to sing some of the verses for my mother. She sang:

En nombre del cielo	In the name of Heaven
Os pido pasada,	I beg you for lodging,
Pues no puede andar	For she cannot walk,
Mi esposa amada.	My beloved wife.

Aquí no es meson;	This is not an inn
Sigan adelante.	So keep going;
No seas inhumano;	Don't be inhuman;
Tennos caridad.	Have mercy on us.

"There are a lot more verses," Martha said. "In the end, Joseph and Mary always get to come in, and that's when we all go inside and have a party."

Before the party, Martha and I helped put candy into a *piñata* that looked like a star. It was pink and blue, and each point had a silver tassel. It was so pretty that I didn't want anyone to break it. "It's supposed to be broken," said Martha.

Martha showed me the nativity scene on a table in the living room. "My grandmother put the poinsettia plants around it. I put the angel by the stable," she said.

I looked at the wooden figures. There was no baby in the manger, and I asked Martha if she had forgotten him. "No, we put the baby Jesus there on Christmas Eve," she said.

When we heard singing outside, Mr. Rodriguez answered the door. Two children were pulling a wagon full of pine branches. There were statues of Mary and Joseph and an angel in it. Some people carried lighted candles. The visitors sang, asking to come in.

Martha and her family sang back and said they had no room. Then they changed their minds and invited the singers to come in.

Mrs. Rodriguez and Alicia gave out thick cookies with raspberry jelly and coconut on top.

"Where's the *piñata*?" I asked Martha.

"In the back yard." she said. "We'll break it as soon as my father says it's time."

When Mr. Rodriguez went outside, all the children followed him. Several children swung at the *piñata* and missed. Then Inez hit a point of the star hard. The whole point fell off and candy spilled out. Martha and I didn't scramble for it like we did on her birthday. We had eaten so much candy while we filled the *piñata* that we couldn't eat any more.

It was two days before Christmas. I went to Martha's house early in the morning because she said I could help make the Christmas tamales.

Martha's mother and grandmother were putting out the things for the tamales. The corn husks were soaking in a big pan. The corn meal mixture was in a pot, and the stuffings were in bowls.

"We'll show you how to make tamales, then you can help," Mrs. Rodriguez said to me. She shook the water off some corn husks and dried them with a towel. She spread a big spoonful of corn meal dough on a corn husk and handed it to cousin Inez.

Alicia and Inez put some chopped pork and green chili pepper on top of the dough and added a fat ripe olive. Martha's grandmother folded the sides of the husk together over the dough and the filling. Then she turned up the bottom and folded the top over it.

"Let me tie this one, it's so full," Alicia said as she tore a strip off a corn husk. She tied the strip around the tamale.

"I want to do the tying," said Martha.

"Okay," said her mother. "Tie them carefully. We don't want the water to get inside when they're steamed."

Mrs. Rodriguez spread the dough on the corn husks, Alicia and her grandmother put in the filling. I got to put the olives in the tamales. Then Inez folded the corn husks and held the tamales closed while Martha tied them.

Abuelita gave Martha a little squeeze and spoke to her. Martha laughed and said, "Abuelita says I'm going to be a good cook because Saint Martha is the patron saint of cooks."

Mrs. Rodriguez put water in the bottom of the steamer pot and lined the top with corn husks. We all helped stack the tamales in the pot.

Martha's grandmother spoke in Spanish. "*Abuela* is telling us to pack them firmly, but leave room for them to swell," said Inez.

Alicia took some dough from another bowl and spread it on some smaller corn husks. "This is sweet dough for the sweet tamales," she said. "I'm putting some sugar sprinkles, a shake of cinnamon, and a couple of nuts and raisins in each one." Her hands worked on the tamales as she talked. She wrapped the husks so the tamales were round and long. She tied a husk tie around each end.

"We can tell the meat and the sweet tamales apart by their shape," Inez said.

When all the tamales were packed in the kettle, Alicia covered them with more corn husks and a heavy lid. Martha and I wanted to taste them. "It will be a long wait," said her mother. "They have to steam for three hours. When these are done, we'll steam the rest. We won't eat them until Christmas Eve. I'll save some for you and your mother, Kathy. But you girls can make tacos with the left overs."

We rolled some meat into flour tortillas. I folded mine like the tamales. Martha laughed and put a husk tie around it.

The next day at my house, I heard the doorbell ring. Javier and Martha were there.

"Hi! Come on in," I said.

"We can't come in," Martha said, "we've got to go right back because everyone's coming to our house for dinner."

"We brought you some tamales," Javier said. Martha held out a basket. It felt heavy when I took it. "There are some meat ones and some sweet ones," she said. There was an embroidered cloth on the top of the tamales.

"Oh thank you. I can't wait to eat them. I'll bring the basket and cloth back to you."

"The cloth's for you to keep," Martha said.

"She did the *punto de cruz*." Javier said.

"He means cross stitch," Martha said.

"That's really neat, Martha. I didn't know you could do that." Pink and red cross stitches made a design like a rose.

"Alicia taught me," Martha said. "I'm glad you like my work."

"I love it! I'll keep it forever," I told her. "Merry Christmas."

❀ 6 ❀
Cousin Luis

After Christmas vacation I waited on the playground for Martha. Finally I saw her. She was walking with a boy I didn't know. I ran to meet her.

"Hi, Kathy. This is my cousin Luis Lopez."

"Hi, Luis," I said.

He held his hand toward me and said, *"Mucho gusto conocerle!"* I felt funny shaking his hand.

"He's from Mexico," Martha said. "He's living with us, and so are his mother and father and sister Yolanda."

I thought about Martha's house that was already so full of people and wondered where the Lopezes would sleep.

Martha answered before I could ask. "They're sleeping in my room. Alicia and I are sleeping on the

couch, Javier is in my parents' room, and Frank is staying with his friend Carlos. He says he doesn't mind because he and Carlos can study together. And they both work at McDonald's."

"Why don't you come and stay at my house?" I asked.

Martha looked at me and smiled. "Thanks, Kathy, but my father wouldn't let me."

"But you're so crowded."

"That's okay. They'll stay with us a while. And then they'll live with Inez's family and then the other aunts and uncles."

"Can you play after school?" I asked.

"Not today. I have to watch Yolanda. She's only a year old."

Luis stood quietly while we talked. "Doesn't he speak any English?" I asked.

"No, and I've got to take him to the office and help him register. Maybe he'll be in our class because Mrs. Sigala speaks Spanish, but he'll still have to take ESL," Martha said.

"What's that?" I asked.

"It's a class where kids who speak Spanish get English lessons. ESL means English as a Second Language."

Martha couldn't visit after school, and I missed her. She said she had to take care of Yolanda and Javier while her mother took Mrs. Lopez around to relatives.

"Why don't you come over on Saturday?" she asked.

On Saturday Martha introduced me to Luis's mother and father. They both shook my hand and said, *"Mucho gusto conocerle."*

As more relatives and friends came, Martha, Luis, and I went out to the back yard. "He's learning English already," Martha said. *"Habla en Inglés, Luis."*

"Hi! My name is Luis. What is your name?" Luis said it like a robot. We all laughed.

Soon the back yard was full of people. They talked in Spanish and hugged each other. Martha saw me staring as her Uncle Bernardo hugged other men as they arrived.

"Men do that in Mexico," she said. "Then they shake hands."

Alicia heard us talking. "It's called an *abrazo*," she said.

Martha laughed and hugged me and patted my back. "Now you've had an *abrazo*."

Alicia said that the Lopezes had waited six years for permission to come to the United States. "Aunt Carmela is my mother's sister. They are so happy to be together again. My father helped Uncle Bernardo get a job at the county airport in the baggage department."

Yolanda was holding onto Alicia's hand and crying. "She wants to be picked up," Alicia said. "Could you take her, Martha? I have to go help in the kitchen."

Martha put Yolanda on her lap and held her hand.

She said a nursery rhyme as she played with her little fingers:

Este se robó un huevo,	This one stole an egg,
Este lo puso a asar,	This one fried it,
Este le echó la sal,	This one put salt on it,
Esta le comió,	This one ate it,
Y este viejo perro	And the old dog
lo fué a chismear.	went and tattled.

"That's like 'This little pig went to market,' " I said, "only that's for toes."

Yolanda held her hand up to Martha and said, *"Más, más."*

"No, Yolanda, no more. Here comes the food."

Mrs. Rodriguez and some of Martha's aunts brought out steaming pots of menudo soup and baskets of warm tortillas and bowls of chopped onions and spices and sliced lemons. The men ate first.

"Help yourselves," Mr. Rodriguez said to us as he pointed to the food.

"Come on, Kathy," said Martha. "Come on Luis." She smiled at him. "Luis got asked to play on the soccer team at school. He played in Mexico, and he's good."

Luis grinned and said, "Soccer, *sí!*"

🌸 **7** 🌸

Cinco de Mayo

We studied about Mexico in social studies this year. Mrs. Sigala, our teacher, asked the class if we would like to have a Mexican *fiesta* at the end of the unit. She suggested we hold it on May fifth. We had learned that May fifth, *Cinco de Mayo,* is a special day in Mexico. People there celebrate because Mexicans won a battle over the French on that day. They're very proud of this victory.

Mrs. Sigala said she'd teach us some dances, and we could sing the songs we'd already learned.

At school the next day Martha was excited. She told the class that her mother would call some of the other mothers and they'd fix a Mexican dinner for everyone to have after the program.

We practiced a lot and finally we were ready to perform the dances for our parents. Some of us danced the *Jarabe Tapatío* (hah-rah-bee TAP-pah-tee-o). It's also called the Mexican Hat Dance because in one part the boys put their hats on the floor and the girls dance around them. "It's the national Mexican folk dance," Mrs. Sigala said.

The girls wore white blouses and green and red skirts. The boys wore jeans and white shirts. Mrs. Sigala said that in Mexico the men dancers dress like the *charros,* in silver-trimmed clothes.

Some of the boys did a dance called *Los Viejitos* (los vee-eh-HEE-tos) which means the little old men. They wore masks that they had made out of paper bags. The masks were painted to look like old men's faces. The boys used walking sticks and danced like stiff old men. Luis was one of these dancers. He was as funny as a clown and made everyone laugh and clap.

While we were dancing the mothers were getting ready to serve Mexican food. They had cooked all afternoon. The smells made us hungry!

Martha said, "They're fixing tacos and enchiladas and beans and rice."

"Why not tamales?" I asked.

"Are you kidding? You know how long they take to fix!"

When we finished dancing, we paraded around the gym. All the parents clapped. Mrs. Sigala led us to the tables by the stage.

"You dancers did such a good job that the mothers want to serve you first," she said.

Martha and I were happy to hear that. "Dancing sure makes me hungry!" she said.

❀ 8 ❀

Las Mañanitas

The second week of May, Martha asked me to spend the night at her house. "I want you to hear my mother's serenade."

She explained that Alicia and some of her friends would get up very early and go to each girl's house and sing *Las Mañanitas* to the mother. It was a special way of observing Mother's Day.

I had never heard a serenade before. And I almost missed this one. Martha began shaking me when it was barely light outside. "Kathy, get up. You're going to miss it."

I rubbed the sleep out of my eyes and went to the door. Alicia and four other girls stood outside holding roses. They began to sing. Their voices sounded pretty in the morning quiet. By the end of the song, Frank, Javier, Martha's father, and Abuelita had joined us at the door. When the girls finished singing, Alicia gave her mother some red roses. Then the girls left to go to another house.

We went out to the kitchen and I helped Martha set the table for breakfast. In a few minutes steaming plates of scrambled eggs and *chorizo* (choh-REE-soh), Mexican sausage, were put on the table with fresh tortillas. Mrs. Rodriguez put her roses in the center of the table so all of us could look at them.

"Thanks, Martha, for inviting me," I said.

I don't often see Martha on Sunday because she is very busy with her family. Each Monday she tells me what she did on Sunday. After mass, they all go to visit *abuelito* in the cemetery. Last week Martha put some paper flowers she had made on his grave. Then they visit her relatives. Martha says visiting sometimes takes all day. Other times they meet friends in the park by the zoo. For a treat she gets a popsicle from the ice cream vendor. Martha says that she gives thanks to God all day Sunday. She says thanks for friends and family, for popsicles, and for seeing the tiger in the zoo.

One afternoon Martha said, "Kathy, do you want to see the pictures of Inez's *quinceañera?* She loaned us her album."

As we looked at the pictures, Martha explained about Inez's special day. "Here's Inez and her attendants. Look here's Alicia. And here's a picture of my family with Inez. She gave us one like this for our picture wall."

"Inez's dress is beautiful," I said. Her long pink satin dress was trimmed with lace and ribbons. She

looked like a princess. "What a way to celebrate her fifteenth birthday."

"My parents bought her that dress because they're her godparents," Martha said. "They also gave her a ring as a special reminder of her day."

Martha turned another page in the album. "The *quinceañera* began in church. Inez's attendants and their escorts walked down the aisle slowly. Then Inez came down the aisle with her parents. She looked just like a bride."

"Look here's Frank in a tuxedo," I said. "He looks uncomfortable." We both laughed.

Martha went on. "The mass was in Spanish. Father Ramon said all kinds of special things about Inez. She was so happy that she cried. Afteward we went to a park. That's where most of these pictures were taken."

There were pages and pages of pictures with Inez and each of her attendants and relatives.

"Then everyone went back to Inez's house," Martha continued. "There were so many relatives. Aunt Martha said we were stuffed in her house like tamales in a pot. You should have seen how much food there was. Everyone brought something to share. Uncle Ernesto barbecued a goat in a pit in the ground."

"A goat?" I said, surprised.

Martha laughed. "It's delicious. It tastes a lot like pork. Uncle dug the pit the day before and lined it with coals. He put the goat meat in and covered it with cactus leaves. The meat cooked slowly until party time."

"What happened next?"

"The music started and Inez danced the first dance with her father, Uncle Ernesto. He looked so proud. He kept talking about Inez all evening. He said he'd dance again at her wedding. He told Inez that he wanted her to have a good young man for a husband. That embarrassed her."

Martha pointed to another picture. "Look at the cake. It was huge. It had six layers. And there were tiny girl and boy dolls on it. They were supposed to be Inez's attendants and escorts."

"I wish I could go to a *quinceañera*," I said.

"Maybe you can. Alicia will be fifteen on her next birthday. And in a few years when I'm fifteen you can be one of my attendants, because you're my best friend."

I gave Martha a big *abrazo*. "You're my best friend, too."

Glossary

abrazo (ah-BRA-zo)   a way people greet each other, hugging and patting each other's backs.

abuelita, abuelito (ah-bay-LEE-tah)   a loving way to say grandmother (abuela) and grandfather (abuelo).

charros (CHAR-rrohs)   expert horsemen who wear the traditional costumes worn by gentleman ranchers.

Cinco de Mayo (SEEN-ko day MAI-oh)   the fifth of May, a holiday celebrating a Mexican victory over the French.

las mañanitas (man-yan-EE-tas)   songs sung during serenades, especially on birthdays.

mariachis (mar-ree-AH-chees)   musicians who dress in charro costumes and sing and play traditional Mexican songs.

mucho gusto conocerle (MU-cho gus-to ko-no-SER-lay)   words that mean "I'm glad to meet you." Sometimes shortened to "mucho gusto."

piñata (pee-NYAH-tah)   a container filled with candy. People break it open with a stick, and then scramble to get the candy.

Las Posadas (po-SAH-das)   nine nights (December 16 to 24) celebrating the search of Mary and Joseph for a place to stay in Bethlehem.

quinceañera (kin-SIN-nyer-ah)   a celebration for a girl on her fifteenth birthday.

Some Books about Mexico

Darbois, Dominique. *Tacho, Boy of Mexico*. Chicago: Follett, 1961.

Epstein, Sam and Beryl. *Mexico, a First Book, Revised Edition*. New York: Franklin Watts, 1983.

Friskey, Maragaret. *Welcome to Mexico*. Chicago: Childrens Press, 1975.

Grant, Clara Louise and Jane Werner Watson. *Mexico, Land of the Plumed Serpent*. Champaign, Illinois: Garrard Publishing Company, 1968.

Lye, Keith. *Take a Trip to Mexico*. London: Franklin Watts, 1982.

Marcus, Rebecca and Judith. *Fiesta Time in Mexico*. Champaign, Illinois: Garrard Publishing Company, 1974.

Stein, R. Conrad. *Mexico*. Chicago: Childrens Press, 1984.

About the Authors

Dianne MacMillan grew up in St. Louis, Missouri, and graduated from Miami University in Ohio with a Bachelor of Science Degree in Education. She taught school for many years but now spends her time writing. Her stories have appeared in textbooks and in many children's magazines such as *Highlights for Children, Jack and Jill,* and *Cobblestone.* She is a member of the Society of Children's Book Writers and lives in Anaheim, California with her husband and three children.

Dorothy Rhodes Freeman is an educator and author of twenty-one books. Four of these are about children whose heritage is Mexican: *Someone for Maria, A Home for Memo, The Friday Surprise,* and *Alfredo, Bernardo, Carlota.* She has designed training for teachers who teach English to Spanish-speaking children. She currently writes bilingual education projects and monitors and evaluates the results. Writing is both her vocation and hobby. She has two grown children and lives with her husband in Placentia, California.